LOOKING AT THE CROSS THROUGH AN OLD TESTAMENT LENS

Studies by Paul Smith

A  Publication

Published on behalf of MET by

MOORLEYS
Print, Design & Publishing
info@moorleys.co.uk · www.moorleys.co.uk

ISBN 978 0 86071 781 2

© Copyright 2019 D Paul Smith and MET

All rights reserved.
No part of this publication may be reproduced, stored in a retrieval system, or transmitted, in any form or by any means, electronic, mechanical, photocopying, recording or otherwise, without the prior written permission of the publishers.

British Library Cataloguing in Publication Data.
A catalogue record for this book is available from the British Library.

Preface

LOOKING AT THE CROSS THROUGH AN OLD TESTAMENT LENS

This little book has been prepared in the hope that it will give you a better understanding of the most profound event in all history – the death of the eternal Son of God, the Lord Jesus Christ. I hope that it will help you to 'get under the skin' of the first followers of Jesus and consider His death as they did. Each episode in this unfolding story will, I trust, enable you to understand the events which influenced both their perception and their interpretation of the story of the Cross.

You can use this book on your own, as part of your devotional programme, or in a house group or study group where you might want to take a different passage each time you meet. Don't rush through the studies. You are not reading a novel. Take time to let the profound truths which the Bible reveals stimulate your mind and set your heart ablaze.

We are not offering a list of questions you are expected to work through, but it might be good to begin by asking, "Is there some truth which I have learned?", "How did this passage of scripture shape the understanding of the first disciples?", "How does it help me understand the work of the cross a little better?", "What is God asking me to do in response to what He has first done for me?"

Draw me nearer, nearer.... to Thy precious bleeding side.

Paul Smith

Contents

	Page
INTRODUCTION	1
1. ABRAHAM'S FAITH IS TESTED Genesis 22:1-19	4
2. THE PASSOVER Exodus 12:1-30	10
3. THE DAY OF ATONEMENT Leviticus 16	16
4. THE SUFFERING SERVANT Isaiah 52:13-53:12	22
5. MY GOD, WHY? Psalm 22	29
AND FINALLY......	36

Methodist Evangelicals Together
is the largest independent organization in British Methodism today, a renewal movement uniting and representing evangelicals at every level within our denomination.

Our three core purposes are:
- **ADVOCATING:** Promoting and representing evangelicalism within Methodism, and Wesleyan evangelicalism within the wider evangelical world.
- **EQUIPPING:** Providing resources through publications, conferences and our website for evangelicals within British Methodism.
- **SUPPORTING:** Offering pastoral support and advice to evangelicals, who can often feel isolated within Methodism and face particular pressures.

MET is a fellowship for every Methodist who shares our desire to:
- Uphold the authority of Scripture
- Seek Spiritual Renewal
- Pray for Revival
- Spread Scriptural holiness
- Emphasise the centrality of the Cross

MET promotes partnership in the Gospel to proclaim Jesus as Lord. Our partners include:
- Cliff College
- ECG
- LWPT
- Share Jesus International
- Inspire Network

Join MET and partner with us to:
- Network with evangelical Methodists in prayer and action.
- Add your voice to 1700 others on key issues at all levels of the Methodist Church and beyond.
- Participate in national and local events.
- Receive the MET Connexion Magazine.

Find us at: www.methodistevangelicals.org.uk

or write to us
c/o Moorleys Print & Publishing, 23 Park Road, Ilkeston, Derbys DE7 5DA
who will pass on your valued enquiry

LOOKING AT THE CROSS
THROUGH AN OLD TESTAMENT LENS

Introduction

I was shaking hands as the congregation left the church one Sunday recently when I had preached on a passage from the Old Testament. After expressing her appreciation for the service one lady looked me straight in the eye and said, "I don't believe in the Old Testament." It was neither the time nor the place to enter into a lengthy discussion about the authority of scripture, so I let her go with that as her parting shot.

What did she mean? She can't have meant that she did not believe it existed; she may have meant that she did not trust it; but I guess she meant that she did not believe that the Old Testament was relevant to her in any way. I think there are a lot of people like that in our churches. The Old Testament seems like a musty book from a very long time ago which contains some good stories but has no real relevance to their lives today. But when we get into the New Testament it's a different matter. That's where the real message is found!

So let's begin this short series of studies by reminding ourselves that the scriptures contained in the Old Testament were the only ones which the first followers of Jesus had. Every time the word 'scripture' is used on the New Testament the people who wrote it, and those who first read it, must have thought of those books which we call the Old Testament because they hadn't got anything else. Furthermore, the number of occasions when the Old Testament is quoted in the New convinces us that those who wrote the New Testament believed that through the history of God's people the Lord had been at work preparing for the coming of His Son. The unfolding story was going somewhere, and the coming of Jesus, in both His teaching and His work, was the fulfilment of all that God had been hinting at for long centuries before.

There are two ways of looking at this. From a human point of view we can say that the way the New Testament writers thought had been conditioned by the history of their nation. So when they thought about what God had done through Jesus they did so as people who knew how God had acted in the past; and they understood His work through Christ according to the principles which had been laid down in the Old Testament narrative. From what we might call the 'God-ward' perspective we can say that through the unfolding narrative of the Old Testament God was moulding and shaping the understanding of His people so that when Christ came those who met Him, heard Him and witnessed His work understood it in the light of what God had taught them.

This is, or course, true of all the ministry of Jesus; but it is supremely true when we consider how the New Testament writers thought about the cross. The way they came to understand that event had been shaped and moulded by their knowledge of God's dealings with His people as recorded in the Old Testament. This was precisely because God had been at work in the history of their nation moulding the thinking of His people, so that when He was to send His Son folk would understand what He was doing.

In this short series we are going to think carefully about five passages from the Old Testament which are of particular significance. There are others which are also influential, but it seems to me that these are of particular importance. As best we can, we will try and look at the Cross of Christ through the lens of the Old Testament, because that is how the first followers of Jesus saw it.

1. ABRAHAM'S FAITH IS TESTED

Genesis 22:1-19

Most of us find this story both fascinating and daunting. We are inspired by Abraham's faith, but we are perplexed by what he was expected to do. The story immediately presents us with a number of problems. The first one is that we know how the story ends. We are over-familiar with it and so the heart wrenching challenge which Abraham faced is lost on us. We know that it all worked out alright in the end.

Another problem concerns the practice of child sacrifice. How on earth could Abraham have sincerely believed that God wanted him to sacrifice his only son? Of course there are those who tell us that this was common practice amongst the people who lived in the area and so Abraham got the idea from them. But that will not do, because the Bible clearly says that God told him to do it. To speak of the influence of those who lived in the area might solve one problem, about child sacrifice, but it creates another about the inspiration and authority of scripture. And after all Abraham is called 'the friend of God'. Would he have got it wrong?

Then there is the sheer absurdity of the command. We know that God's promise to Abraham is that through his offspring all the nations of the earth would be blessed. We also know how unlikely it was that he and Sarah would have a child at their age. It was absurd. There were one or two false starts, but eventually God kept His promise and Isaac was born. How can it be that this same God would now ask Abraham to sacrifice his son, and by so doing eliminate the possibility of God's promise being fulfilled?

It's a difficult story, but a very important one. So I want us to think about it in two ways. We will first of all stand up close to it and observe some of the details and then we'll stand back a bit and try to see this story as part of the unfolding picture of redemption which the Bible paints.

We need to be careful to observe exactly what the Bible says, and what it does not say. As the story begins we are told that 'God tested Abraham'. That is to say, God knew how this would end even though Abraham had no idea. What makes Abraham's faith so admirable is that he obeyed when he did not know the end of the story. He simply said, 'Here I am.' And when God told him to do it, he did it. He trusted God when he could not work it out. His whole life had been built on the promise which God had made to make of his descendants a great nation, and now he was being asked to sacrifice the one whereby that promise might be fulfilled. No wonder he had a problem. But the problem did not prevent him trusting in a God who would work it out in the end, and acting in obedience to such a God.

I wonder if this resonates with your experience. Have there been times in your life when you have been perplexed about the way God seems to have been speaking to you? Speaking for myself I can recall occasions when I have felt the call of God in a particular direction. I have prayed about it and the sense of calling has grown deeper. I have 'put down a fleece' and that too has seemed to confirm the call. I have spoken to trusted Christian friends and they too have endorsed my growing conviction. But then, after I have tried to be as obedient as I could, it has not worked out. Did I get it wrong? Maybe. Was I right to act in simple obedience to the will of God as I understood it? Certainly. Yet I have learned that all the while I need to keep trusting that God will work it out – even when I cannot see the way ahead, or even more difficult, find the way ahead confusing.

To return to the story – we are given a little insight into Abraham's attitude as we read in verse 5 that Abraham tells the servants that he and Isaac will worship 'and then *we* will come back to you'. So he must have known that God would somehow keep His promise, despite his apparently contradictory command. The writer of the Epistle to the Hebrews helps us here. In chapter 11 where he is listing the great examples of faith in the Old Testament he refers to this very episode in Abraham's life in verses 17-19. It is there that we are told 'Abraham reasoned that God could raise the dead...' So he knew that even though it was most confusing to him, God would work it out. And I guess that's what we have to do too.

We ought not to miss the point that, from this very early date, worship involves sacrifice. That too is a difficult concept for some people to grasp; but this is how the Bible sees it. To come into the presence of God is an awesome thing. He cannot be approached on a whim, just when we feel like it, as though He were a convenience. He is holy, and we are sinners. Indeed one could argue that the chief message of the whole Bible concerns how sinners can come into the presence of a holy God. In the Old Testament the answer was by way of sacrifice. Blood had to be shed. A life had to be offered up if worship was to be acceptable to God.

So off they go, this little procession, initially four and then just Abraham and Isaac. Abraham is carrying the fire and the knife and Isaac is carrying the wood on which he is to die. But he does not know that, so the question comes 'where is the lamb?' To which Abraham replies 'God Himself will provide'. Again in verse 14, when the story is coming to an end, Abraham is so impressed by God's provision that he names the place 'Jehovah Jireh'– the Lord will provide. And God did. A ram caught by its horns became the sacrifice instead and Isaac was saved. Abraham had passed the test. Isaac was saved. God was honoured and Abraham's faith was vindicated.

There are one or two other details which we need to note in just a moment but we are in a position now to stand back and see this story, initially at least, in the stream of Biblical revelation. What is God doing here to shape the understanding of His people? And how did that influence the way in which the first followers of Jesus thought about the cross?

It lodged in their minds the understanding of substitution; the ram died in place of Isaac. In later studies we will come across this again, but we can note at this point that from this very early date in the unfolding story the people of God came to realise that one life could be saved by another life being lost. Or to put it another way – one life could be kept by another life being offered. So when the first followers of Jesus began to reflect on the cross of Christ it was quite natural for them to think of Him dying instead of another. His life was offered so that the life of another might be saved. We are not suggesting that this is the only valid way that they thought about the cross; but we are suggesting that it was an obvious conclusion for them to draw because of their religious heritage. Surrender of one life means salvation for another.

The other details which we need to observe shed even more light on the subject. One of them is simple and the other a little more complicated. Let's deal with the complicated one first.

The Septuagint was a translation of the Old Testament from Hebrew and Aramaic into Greek. Tradition has it that it was conducted by 70 scholars; hence its name and the fact that it is often abbreviated as LXX. It is a very important document because it enables us to make a comparison with the Greek of the New Testament and indicates clearly the correct translation of the Hebrew, as the translators understood it. When we read this passage in the Septuagint we find that the word 'only' in verses 2 and 12 is translated into the Greek word which is, in the New Testament, translated 'beloved'. So verse two reads *'Take your son, your beloved son….'* And verse 12 reads *'….because you have not withheld from me your son, your beloved son.'* You will recall that this is how God the Father refers to the Lord Jesus on a number of occasions within the Gospels.

Now for the other detail – Why did the writer of Genesis think it was worth recording who carried what as this procession made its way to the place of sacrifice? Does it not seem rather odd to make it clear that Abraham carried the fire and the knife but he, the father, placed the wood on his son. Isaac carried the wood on which he was to be sacrificed. If you had been telling this story is this a level of detail which you would have recorded? Probably not. Then why was it recorded here? Could it be that several millennia before it happened God was giving a fore-shadowing of what was to happen later to the Lord Jesus?

When we take all these things together we discover how important this story really is. We have the requirement of sacrifice if we are to come into the presence of a holy God. We also have the establishment of the idea of substitution which points us forward to the passion and death of Christ. The beloved son is taken. He carries the wood on which he is to be sacrificed to the place where the execution is to take place. It is not because the father does not love the son. It is simply because there was no other way.

When I ask people why they think Jesus died they come up with all sorts of answers. Some say that it was to obtain our forgiveness and others talk about reconciliation. And if I ask who was responsible I get different answers again. Some talk about the Romans, others about the prejudice of the Jewish authorities or the betrayal of Judas, or the fact that the disciples all ran away. Whilst all that may in a sense be true there must be a deeper reason. After all Jesus says that the very reason for His coming was *'to give His life a ransom for many'*. When everyone was warning Him not to go to Jerusalem it only strengthened His resolve. It is as though He had an appointment to keep. So we are forced into the uncomfortable truth that Jesus was not the victim in all this. He was the architect. There simply was no other way. The Father laid the wood on His Son. The Son carried it. The sacrifice was made. The substitution was complete. The innocent dies and the guilty go free. It's called grace!

2. THE PASSOVER

Exodus 12:1-30

It would be difficult to over-state the importance of the Passover celebrations for the Jewish nation. They were given a tangible way of recalling, indeed re-enacting, what God had done in setting them free from bondage in Egypt. The Passover was without doubt one of the foundation stones on which the Jewish understanding of their relationship with God was built. For the Christian too this is of supreme importance. It was at the Passover meal that the Lord's Supper was instituted. Despite the threatening clouds of opposition Jesus seems to be determined to go to Jerusalem for the Passover festival. He arranges for the preparations to be made. He seems to consider it important that His own death ought to occur against the background of the Passover celebrations, as though the latter would help His people understand the former. Indeed, that is how His first followers came to think of His sacrifice on Calvary. Paul speaks of Christ as our *'Passover Lamb'* (1 Corinthians 5:7). So if we are to think about the Cross of Christ from an Old Testament perspective it is really important that we give serious consideration to the Passover.

Let's begin by recalling the events which led to this decisive moment. The Jewish nation had been held in bondage in Egypt. God called Moses with the specific ministry of going to Pharaoh with God's command, "Let my people go." You will recall Pharaoh's disobedience, with the result that a number of plagues were sent to persuade him to change his mind. On each occasion Pharaoh refused to listen until eventually the last of the plagues was sent – the death of the firstborn. On a predetermined night God would pass through Egypt and 'strike down' every firstborn, both humans and animals. It is against this background that the Passover meal was instituted.

I guess most of us are familiar with the story, but the danger with familiarity is that we think we know it and so we miss the all-important details. If we are to get to the heart of this it is important to examine the story carefully. For example, we need to identify the contrast between this last plague and all those which went before. For one thing all the previous plagues were mediated by Moses, or Aaron, or both of them together. They were to go to Pharaoh and tell him what God would do if he remained intransigent and disobedient to God's will. So these plagues were designed to get Pharaoh to change his mind. The last plague, the death of the firstborn, is different. Here Moses and Aaron do not act as mediators, God just does it. Here God is not acting to persuade Pharaoh to change his mind. Here God is acting in judgement because of Pharaoh's earlier disobedience. It is very clear from verse 12. God says *'I will pass through Egypt…..and will bring judgement on all the gods of Egypt.'*

Once we grasp this very important detail it changes our whole perspective on the story. Here we are encountering a God who has acted in grace and mercy, in that He has given Pharaoh many opportunities to change his mind; but when those opportunities are refused God acts in judgement. I wonder when you last heard a sermon on the judgement of God, or how often you have noticed this as an emphasis in the hymns and worship songs we sing? Today we tend to stress God's grace and mercy for sinners. Maybe this story comes as a timely reminder that no one can expect to stand against a holy God and ultimately get away with it. Judgement is God's alternative to mercy, where that mercy is persistently refused.

If we miss this initial, crucial detail we are in danger of misunderstanding the remainder of the story; but to grasp this enables us to get to the truth which the rest of the story offers. It changes everything about the way we understand it.

It presents us with the question, "When God acts in judgement who can stand before Him?" After all, we are all sinners. We have all refused the mercy of God. We have all denied His rightful Lordship in our lives, living for self instead of living for Him. We have all had other god's; different from theirs but just as potent in usurping the Lord's rightful place in our lives. We used to sing

> "Eternal light, eternal light, how pure the soul must be,
> When placed within Thy searching sight,
> It shrinks not, but, with calm delight,
> Can live and look on Thee?
>
> O how shall I, whose native sphere is dark, whose mind is dim,
> Before the Ineffable appear,
> And on my naked spirit bear
> The uncreated beam?"

On that night in Egypt everyone stood under the judgement of God, for they had all refused His will in one way or another; both Egyptians and Jews. So the question is 'How can we escape the judgement of God?' This is where we get to the specific instructions which were given to the Jewish people. They were to slaughter a lamb, catch its blood and spread it on the doorposts and the lintel of their homes. This was the way they were to escape God's judgement. When this story is told it is often presented as though this was the way the Jewish people were to distinguish their homes from those of the Egyptians. But when you think about it such a suggestion is ludicrous. Do we really believe that the creator of the universe was not aware of their addresses?! It cannot be that God did not know where they lived. There must be some other explanation. We find it in verse 12 *"When I see the blood, I will pass over you"*. It was the blood which changed God's attitude to the people. They could escape the judgement of God because of the blood of the lamb; because the lamb died they could be set free.

Let's be quite clear about it. On that night in Egypt there was a death in *every* home. (see verse 30) It was either the death of the lamb or the death of the firstborn. The firstborn, in the homes which displayed that blood, was saved because the lamb had died. The blood was essential. The issue becomes clear when we ask what would have happened if there had been a Jewish home where they had not followed these instructions. Would the judgement of God have been averted? No. God knew where they lived, but that was not the issue; for without the blood they all stood under the judgement and condemnation of a holy God. It was the blood which made the difference.

Further, the regulations concerning the selection of the lamb were very important. Not any lamb would do. It was not as though some shrewd person could see this as a way of getting rid of the weakling of the flock. It had to be perfect. And the timings were calculated to ensure that after the lamb had been selected there had to be a period when it was held under close scrutiny to ensure that it had not developed some illness with the result that something less than perfect was offered. Only the best is good enough for God.

Nor could a family choose a large lamb in the hope that once the sacrifice had been made they could use the rest as a ready supply of meat for the rest of the week! If the lamb was too large, families had to come together to eat it. Similarly if the family was too small to consume the whole lamb on their own they were to share it with their nearest neighbour. Why are the regulations so precise? It is to ensure that the people understood that the whole purpose of that lamb was not to feed the family for the week but to give its life to avert the judgement of God on the occupants of that household. Its sole purpose was to die. Through its death it provided a way of salvation for all those whose numbers and needs it matched.

Similar detailed instructions were given to those who were to eat the meal, concerning both their attire and the way they were to eat it. Even though it was to be eaten at the end of the day it was not to be eaten in a relaxed manner, as one would normally eat an evening meal with the family, but in haste; as though time was running out. Nor could they wear the kind of clothing associated with a relaxing evening together; they had to be ready to go. Slippers were out and walking boots were in! For those who first participated in this meal these instructions must have come as a shock. They were slaves, bound in servitude; but they were to behave as though they were free. God's promise was so secure that their behaviour was to anticipate the time when it would actually be fulfilled.

For many of us, I guess, a major challenge is to establish in our minds the relationship between the instructions given and the result that all this was designed to accomplish. How on earth can the death of a lamb, or the clothing you wear result in slaves becoming free men and women? It defies our logic. But it must have been the same, or even more acute, for them. Yet they were not called to grasp it all, to fully understand what was going on. They were just called to be obedient to God's will, and by so doing demonstrate their trust in Him and His purposes for them. Their obedience evidenced their faith. The unfolding history of their nation reveals that later, as they had time to reflect on these momentous events, they could see things clearer; but at the time their obedience was a simple act of faith. That's how it has to be for us too. The promise of God, the blood of the lamb and the obedient faith of the people come together to result in slaves being set free, lives being transformed and God's purposes being fulfilled.

Having thought about this story in this way it must come as no surprise to us that when those who first encountered Jesus came to reflect on the work of the cross they saw it through a Passover lens. He is called 'The Lamb of God'. He dies at Passover time. By His own admission this is why He came. We are even told that the herb used to spread the blood on the doorposts and lintel was the same one used to elevate a sponge to the lips of the dying Saviour as He hung on the cross (John 19:29). It all begins to fit. There is no doubt that when the New Testament writers came to reflect on the cross they understood quite clearly that what God had done for His people long ago through the death of a lamb, He had now done for everyone through the death of His Son, just as it was for them so long ago. The aversion of God's judgement, the blessings of those who are really free to be the people He can make them, are appropriated not by understanding, but by a simple faith that takes God at His word and demonstrates faith with obedience.

3. THE DAY OF ATONEMENT

Leviticus 16

Like the Passover festival, the Day of Atonement is of particular importance as we consider the influence the Old Testament had on those who first tried to understand the cross of Christ. But unlike the Passover it is seldom the focus of Christian thought or devotion today. When did you last hear a sermon from Leviticus 16? So we need to give it our careful consideration if we are to grasp its influence on the first followers of Jesus.

Let's begin by setting the scene. The instructions are given to Moses *'after the death of the two sons of Aaron'* (v1). We find a record of this event in Leviticus 10. A detailed study would help our understanding, but let it be sufficient at this stage to say that their attitude and behaviour had not given the respect and honour due to a holy God. They had not observed the required regulations. In short, they had barged into the presence of God when and as they wanted, rather than as God required. The regulations concerning the Day of Atonement are given against that background. What does it take for unworthy sinners to come into the presence of a holy God and still stand?

Further, it will help our understanding if we remind ourselves of the layout of the tabernacle where worship was offered. We can read the details of both the Tabernacle and the priestly garments in Exodus 26-28. It makes interesting reading, despite what you may think! After all, they were a people on the move. The Tabernacle was a portable structure. Every time they camped in a new place it had to be erected, and every time they broke camp it had to be packed up for the journey. You may be surprised by the dimensions. It must have been quite a job. You can also read the details of what the priest was required to wear. They are very specific.

Now why is this all so important? Precisely because it helps us to understand how these people regarded the God whom they worshipped. More than anything else He was holy. You could not barge into His presence just when you wanted. To treat Him with disrespect was a very serious matter. Everything had to be just right if your worship was to be acceptable. You may want to reflect for a moment on how this relates to the common attitude to worship today in so many of our churches. We think it is there for our convenience. I am thinking of the gentleman who shook me by the hand at the end of one service, looked me straight in the eye and said, "It didn't do much for me!" I just smiled, but as he walked away I felt like shouting, "That's not what it was designed to do!" We are not arranging a concert. We are offering worship and our first priority must always be to offer something worthy of the One who we worship. It is then that the Lord 'inhabits the praises of His people'. It is then that they encounter Him and are changed by Him.

All this is reinforced when we understand the layout of the Tabernacle. There were a number of different areas within the perimeter, but right at its heart there was what is now called the Most Holy Place, and is later called the Holy of Holies. This is where God is, and if you are to encounter Him you will encounter Him there. But bearing in mind all that we have said about God's holiness the pertinent question is 'What needs to be done in order to enter the Most Holy Place? What needs to happen for sinners to encounter and have a relationship with God?' That is the context for the Day of Atonement.

The short answer is that sin needs to be dealt with in some way. Atonement needs to be made for it. Which in turn leads us on to other questions. What is sin? What is atonement? How is atonement obtained?

We may just use the word 'sin' and think we know what we mean by it, but the Biblical writers were much more precise. As you read Leviticus 16 you will find number of different words used, and each one brings its own shade of meaning. The word 'uncleanness' brings with it the idea of spiritual pollution or contamination, a concept which is foreign to most of us but was real for them. This explains why atonement had to be made for things as well as people. Articles and places could be contaminated by sin, by being touched by sinners, or in an unworthy way, so atonement needed to be made for them too. Then there is the word 'rebellion' which signifies a deliberate act; deciding against the will of God. 'Wickedness' is about the perversion of human nature, our tendency to prefer the bad rather than the good. And the word 'sin' is a kind of catch-all word, frequently used in this chapter, which describes any act or disposition which is contrary to the will of God, conscious or unconscious. Given that comprehensive catalogue no one can doubt that we are all sinners and stand under the condemnation of a holy God.

The word 'atonement' describes what it takes to put this right. Rather simplistically some have understood this as at-one-ment. That is to say: What needs to be done to re-establish the relationship between the sinner and the one sinned against? There are at least two dimensions to the question. We can regard it as a purely legal matter. In which case we would say, for example, if someone breaks the law they ought to be punished for it. Society is unable to function effectively if people can go around breaking the law and not having to face any consequences for doing so. It offends our sense of morality. So those who regard atonement in that way will speak of atonement being effected when the price is paid for sin, and in this case the victim is the animal, bull, sheep or goat. I am able to escape the consequences of my sin because the animal bears the penalty for it.

All this is true, but it is only half the story. Maybe an illustration will help. Let us imagine a rather wayward young person who steals from an old lady. He is caught, convicted and the just deserts of the law are met by the sentence which he completes. When he is released, or when the fine is paid – whatever it might be, the price has been paid and atonement for his sin has been made. But let us imagine that the old person from whom he stole was his grandmother. This throws a whole new light on the situation. When the sentence has been completed atonement may have been completed in one respect, but there is another dimension to it now. A relationship needs to be healed as well. Now it is not just a legal matter, it is relational as well. This is very important here. Throughout the Bible atonement is not just about a legal transaction. It is about healing a broken relationship with God.

So how did all this work out on the Day of Atonement? Of course, Aaron is a sinner too, so he has to make atonement for his own sin before he can do so for the people. Further, remember what we said earlier about sin being like a contamination which can infect things as well as people, he needs to make atonement for all the holy objects which have been polluted by sin. Only then can he make atonement for the people.

In each case sacrifice is required; a young bull and a ram for Aaron's own sin and then two goats for the sin of the people. After slaughtering the bull he is to take some of the blood and sprinkle it on various artefacts to purify them, the atonement cover, the horns of the altar, etc. Once he has done this he is able to make atonement for the sins of the people. This involves two goats, one is slaughtered and the other becomes the scapegoat, driven into the wilderness. So we note once again that the shedding of blood, the offering up of a life, is required to both pay the penalty for sin and restore the broken relationship. It is also significant that the priest, first on his own behalf and that of his household and secondly on behalf of the people, is to identify with the animal which is to be slaughtered. He lays his hands upon it. It is a powerful picture of identification with the victim. The guilt and consequences of his sin are placed on the animal. The animal bears the penalty, sin is forgiven because the price has been paid; and the relationship is restored because the sin has been dealt with. There is now no obstacle to the relationship.

The involvement of two goats in this ritual brings a new and powerful dimension to the story. The one goat dies to bear the penalty for sin whilst the other is led into the wilderness never to return. It is a dramatic ritual demonstration of what is actually happening to sin. In the one case the life is offered to pay a price and in the other the sins of the people are laid on the goat who then takes them away for ever.

Let's just pause in our examination of this narrative for a moment as we try and grasp its relevance for us today. Many people live with regret, guilt and shame. The past seems to have a tight grip of the soul. They long to be free, but can never quite escape the memory which haunts them. Would it not be wonderful if the slate could be wiped clean, not by burying the past or keeping the door securely locked with the skeleton behind it, but by really dealing with it once and for all? Whatever we may make of this story today, that is how this was seen by God's people of old. Once a year it was an opportunity to come clean with God. They knew the liberty which comes when the price of sin has been paid and when the impediment to a relationship which it creates was taken away.

When we turn to the New Testament we find that this ritual is applied to the work of Christ more explicitly in Hebrews 9 than anywhere else. In fact this chapter provides a commentary on the passage we have been considering. Christ is seen as both priest and victim. Sinless as He was He did not need to make atonement for His own sin as Aaron had done, but became the sacrifice for the sins of the people, paying the price for sin and restoring a broken relationship with God. He *'entered the Most Holy Place once for all, by his own blood'* (Hebrews 9:12) and the writer of Hebrews goes on to speak of the blood of goats and bulls effecting outward cleansing for those on whose behalf it was offered. But he concludes,

> *'How much more then will the blood of Christ.... cleanse our consciences from acts that lead to death so that we may serve the living God'* (Hebrews 9:14)

Our dustbin men make their rounds on Monday mornings. On Sunday afternoon I gather together all the waste and on the following day they come and take it away. Wouldn't it be wonderful if we could just gather all the rubbish in our lives and someone would take it away once and for all. The cross says, 'there is Someone who can do that. He died to take it away for ever.'

4. THE SUFFERING SERVANT

Isaiah 52:13-53:12

As we considered the scapegoat at the end of our last study we observed that through the wonder of Christ's atonement He is able to take away the guilt of His people, like the scapegoat, never to be found again. The question before us now is 'How does He do this?' and the answer is plain; 'He does it through suffering.'

The passage before us is one of the so called 'Servant Songs' of Isaiah's prophecy. There has been much speculation amongst scholars regarding the identity of the Servant. Who did the prophet have in mind as he spoke? Some have suggested that he was speaking of Cyrus, others a small band of faithful people who maintained their trust in the Lord despite all the challenges they had to face. Still others have suggested one of the Kings of Israel or Jeremiah whilst others have suggested a combination of these. In a measure all this may be true, but none of these fulfil the description before us now. The Servant of Isaiah 53 surpasses them all.

On a desert road an Ethiopian official was reading this passage of scripture, but like some of us, he was confused by the identity of the central character. It was just in that moment, in the providence of God, that Philip turned up and answered the question for both the Ethiopian and for us. Luke tells us *'Then Philip began with that very passage of Scripture and told him the good news about Jesus'* (Acts 8:35). So it is clear that from this very early date in the history of the Church the character of Isaiah 53 has been identified with Christ. Indeed we could confidently say that here we have one of the clearest prophetic descriptions of the person and work of our Lord. We may marvel that such a clear description was given so many years before, but for the first followers of Jesus it provided a glorious commentary on who Christ was, what He had come to do and how He accomplished this ministry. When they wanted a clear statement of the gospel from their scriptures this is where they went. They really did look at the cross through this lens. In a way it brings together so much of what we have observed so far in these studies. Here we have echoes of the Day of Atonement and the guilt offering. Here also we have a sacrifice, this time not of a lamb or a goat, but of a human being. The Servant offers Himself for the sin of the people.

How is God going to deal with sin and, at the same time, not contradict His very character of righteousness? How is He able to replace the pattern of guilt and punishment with forgiveness and compassion? The answer lies with His Servant who takes the consequences of sin upon Himself, even though He was innocent. As we reflect on this passage we will see how easy it was for the first followers of Jesus to identify the Servant as the one whom they had come to know as their Saviour.

Let's simply reflect on this passage of scripture, make one or two observations and identify the similarity of the Servant with our Lord Jesus Christ.

Even as this Servant Song begins (52:13-15) we are confronted with an enigma. He will act wisely and receive adulation and praise. He will have an international influence and silence monarchs. Yet this is not for the usual reasons. Indeed, the very one who is so influential will be the one with whom people will be appalled – a very strong word. Here is no celebrity culture. Instead of being the kind of person whose appearance is flaunted before adoring followers he will be one whose appearance is so disfigured that people do not want to look at him. Yet, somehow the most influential in society grasp the truth, about him and because of him.

Here is a message which is unheard of (53:1). Who would have thought it?! Someone who is both vulnerable and ordinary, with no esteem or natural qualities which may allure others, who instead of admiration receives rejection, someone who is despised, not knowing the blessing of God but familiar with sorrow and suffering; he is the Servant of God. Exactly the opposite from what we want to expect, especially in a society which saw material prosperity as a sign of God's favour and suffering as a sign of God's displeasure. Here is one who, it seems, suffers total rejection. His vulnerability, his appearance, the lot life had dealt him, all lead to him being the kind of person from whom others turn away.

Yet in his life there is a greater purpose. His mission does not conform to the popular perception of greatness, but he is the one who is able to deal with humanity's biggest problem. The popular view of suffering being the result of God's judgement on sinners (see John 9:1-12), means that this suffering Servant was perceived to be smitten by God (v4). Yet the truth is that he was smitten, but not for his own sin. It was our iniquities and transgression which resulted in him being pierced, smitten and afflicted. His was the punishment due to us. We are made whole by what happened to him. We are at peace because of what he suffered. Here is vicarious suffering at its most costly.

We ought to pause a moment to consider that phrase *'by his wounds we are healed'* (53:5). It has been much debated and each one of us will have to consider it for ourselves. Let's be clear about the issue – Is healing part of the atonement? There are those who suggest it is and they often use this as a proof-text to argue their position. He not only died that we might be completely forgiven, they say, but also that we might be completely healed. Sin and suffering are spoken of together and Christ is seen as the answer to both. He died, they say, that both might be dealt with.

I think it would clarify the issue if we made some clear statements about this matter. *Firstly*, we need to be clear that God does heal people today. Healing is seen as being a gift of the Spirit. Many today can testify to the way God heals; sometimes in an apparently miraculous way and sometimes through what we like to call medical treatment. But that does not mean some healing is from God and some from the doctors. In the struggle between health and sickness God has, not least through Christ, declared Himself on the side of health. He is the author of it all, whether those who He uses to bring it about recognise Him or not. The God and Father of our Lord Jesus Christ wants to make people whole in every way including physically. *Secondly*, we need to affirm that one day all His people will all be transformed into the people He wants them to be. He will, one day, wipe every tear from our eyes. Death and pain will be no more. On resurrection morning there will be no disease. No more infirmity. Spectacles and Zimmer frames belong to the world that is passing away and they will no longer be required in the new earth which He has promised. So I can, with assurance tell His people that whatever their sickness or disease they will one day be healed.

The question is, therefore, when can I expect that complete physical healing which He has promised? Is it mine today in the same way that complete forgiveness can be mine today? Is it part of the atonement? You must consider this question for yourselves; but speaking for myself I am driven to the conclusion that we are living in 'in between' times. We are saved, but in a way it is only partial salvation. We are made new in Christ, but not completely new this side of resurrection morning. I can promise all who suffer that if they belong to Christ one day they will suffer no more, but I cannot promise them that now. There are a lot of sick saints. Their walk with God is not in question, but they still are crushed under a load of suffering. Sometimes God's answer to the problem of pain is not to take it away. Not just yet. But to transform it into something which points others to one who is able to sustain us no matter what life may throw at us. The most powerful witnesses for Christ are not those for whom life has always been good and exciting, but those who have born suffering, pain and disappointment and shone through it all with the love of God. They have discovered that in the cross Christ took the worst and made that very thing a symbol of hope and sustaining love for every generation which followed. And they have concluded that if He can do that with the horror of Calvary, then He can probably do it with their suffering too. And He has!

We need to make one further point before we move on – to see physical healing as part of the atonement has a very unfortunate side effect for many people. Let us imagine that someone is ill, a Christian prays for them and then they get better. It is very easy for them to see their healing as part of the atonement. They may even quote this verse as a testimony to what God has done. But imagine that physical healing does not come. What effect does that have on them? Too often it compounds their suffering by adding guilt to it. Why is it not working for me? What have I done to prevent the atonement being effective in my case? To them we need to say very clearly, "It is not about what you have done. One day you will be healed. With all God's people you will be whole on resurrection morning. But we live in a fallen world. Bad things do happen to good people. We do not understand it. But we do know that it will not be like this for ever. And we know that it is not because you have done anything wrong or lack faith. We also know that if you offer your suffering to God He will take it and use it for His glory, just as He did with the cross on which His Son died. If He can take the cross, the most brutal form of execution, and make it into the central symbol of the Christian faith; then surely He can do something with my suffering if I offer it to Him."

Let's return to the passage. It is clear that this saving work of the Servant is necessary for us all because, like sheep, we have all gone astray. The essence of sin is turning to our own way, putting self at the centre, regarding other people and circumstances as though they are to be used for your own ends. This is the iniquity which needs to be dealt with. This is what was laid on Him. So it's not just about what we have done. It is about who we are. That's the major problem. Human nature needs to be transformed.

When we read verses 7-9 it is easy to see why the first followers of Jesus thought of this passage as they considered the cross. Here is a perfect description of His death. It was voluntary, like a lamb led to the slaughter, or a sheep which yields to the one who shears it. His death was violent, and bloody. It was all so unfair, to see a life like that ended in such a way. Even when He was dead He was buried like a common criminal; a blameless life discarded in the most violent way, as though no one cared. Why? How do we make sense of it all? The only way is to understand the truth as scripture reveals it. God affirms '*It was for the transgression of my people*' (53:8). That's why it happened. It was not because the religious or civil authorities condemned Him. It was not because He could not do anything about it. It was because this was the answer to a broken world and broken lives, God's answer, and therefore the only answer.

As we approach the end of this 'Servant song' we see that all is not lost. Indeed, through this apparently meaningless death everything was gained. Familiar as the writer was with the sacrificial system he sees the death of the Servant as a guilt offering, given in accordance with God's will. Yet even so he will see the result of his suffering, his offspring, those who benefit from his death. He will be vindicated, by the blessing which results from his suffering, by God, and by countless ones who will be justified because of his sacrificial death. As a consequence he will be counted among the great ones whose lives have brought God's redeeming grace to countless numbers. And all because he offered his life, was obedient unto death, was counted amongst those he came to redeem and took their sin upon himself. He fulfils God's will, meets human being's greatest need and conquers the enemy.

We began this study by acknowledging the speculation there has been about the identity of the Suffering Servant. We end by being as sure as Philip was, so many years ago, on that desert road. There is no doubt – here is the good news about Jesus.

5. MY GOD, WHY?

Psalm 22

As those who are seeking to look at the cross of Christ through an Old Testament lens it is good to remind ourselves that in the passion narratives recorded in the Gospels there are 13 direct quotes from the Old Testament. Of these 9 come from the Psalms and of those 5 come from this Psalm. Clearly this is a very important passage of scripture for us to consider. Of the words of Jesus recorded as He hung on the cross the so-called 'Cry of Dereliction' is a direct quote from the first verse of this Psalm.

This observation presents us with a further question – Did the Father of our Lord Jesus Christ really forsake His Son when He died on the cross? There are those who maintain that He did not; for, they say, God has promised never to forsake His people, let alone His Son. Jesus must have just felt like that. Further, some will point out that whilst the Psalm begins with the cry of dereliction it ends with an affirmation of praise to God for His deliverance. It was Jesus' intention, they maintain, to recite the whole Psalm, but He died before He got to the end.

But such an explanation will not do. It misses the whole point. In fact it misses two points. Firstly it misses the awful consequence of human sin. The tragedy of sin is that it breaks relationships. We see that when we think about human beings. To cheat and lie and deceive someone severs relationships between the one who sins and the one who is sinned against. This is true of our relationship with God. The simple fact is that a holy God cannot tolerate sin. The worst thing about sin is not what it does to other people, or even to ourselves, but what it does to our relationship with God. We cannot be at one with God when are involved with sin. If, as Isaiah 53 maintains, *'the Lord has laid on him the iniquity of us all'* (Isaiah 53:6), Jesus took this awful consequence of sin as well. We cannot have it both ways. Either He did not bear our sin and was mistaken when He uttered the cry of dereliction or He did bear our sin and suffered the awful consequence of doing so. He really was forsaken by the Father.

But there is another reason for maintaining that Jesus really was forsaken. It is that this is what suffering does to people; and not just suffering. Many who have walked this way before us speak of what they often call 'the dark night of the soul'. God is far away. Sometimes it happens through suffering, sometimes through the experiences we have to endure, sometimes for reasons unknown. But for whatever reason there is a period of spiritual depression. Quite apart from the clear references to the passion and death of Christ, here we have a Psalm written by someone going through such a time. It is the experience of a righteous man struggling with the absence of God. Just when you need God most He is farthest away. The Psalmist knows the truth, but it just doesn't seem to fit his experience, and this is made worse by the fact that all those around him seem to 'get it'.

This is far from uncommon amongst Christians today. There was a time when their faith burned brightly, but now simply believing is a strain. Maybe hopes have been dashed, or tragedy has hit us; for whatever reason it is far more difficult to sing God's praises now than once it was. So often this situation is compounded by being amongst others for whom it all seems to work perfectly. We go to church, or to a large Christian gathering, and everyone else seems to be lost in worship but it leaves us feeling cold. What is happening around us does not correspond to what is happening within us. The dark night of the soul is ours. We may believe the right things, but our experience does not correspond to our belief; and to be amongst others who don't have a problem makes our problem worse.

On June 27th 1766 John Wesley wrote to his brother Charles, his confidant, quoting a former letter in the following words

> 'I do not feel the wrath of God abiding on me; nor can I believe it does. And yet (this is the mystery) I do not love God. I never did. Therefore I never believed in the Christian sense of the word. Therefore I am only an honest heathen, a proselyte of the Temple, And yet to be so employed of God! and so hedged in that I can neither get forward nor backward! Surely there never was such an instance before, from the beginning of the world! If I ever have had that faith, it would not be so strange. But I never had ....And yet I dare not preach otherwise than I do, either concerning faith, or love, or justification, or perfection. And yet I find rather an increase than a decrease of zeal for the whole work of God and every part of it.'

If we compare this letter with his Journal we see that at that very time he was in Cumbria, getting up at four, engaging in correspondence, preaching the gospel, and seeing God use him to bring ordinary people to Christ. He was being used of God, yet deep within he felt forsaken and alone.

This tension between truth and experience lies at the heart of this Psalm and must therefore lie at the heart of our interpretation of it. A brief analysis of the Psalm may help us get the point.

If we read the Psalm right through we notice a distinct change in tone between verses 21 and 22. The second half is far more positive than the first. In the second half we have an expression of confidence in God and hope for the world. But the first half is very different. Here the tension between truth and experience is paramount. Indeed, the Psalmist alternates between the two; v1-2 are about his experience, v3-5 about the truth, v6-8 experience, v9-11 truth, v12-18 experience, v19-21 truth.

And if we consider the experiences we could say that -
v1-2 Why? He is forsaken and his prayer is not being heard
v6-8 He is loathed by others, mocked, a lack of self-confidence
v12-18 He laments his condition, immersed in self-pity and exhaustion.

Yet interspersed with that we have affirmations of the truth –
v3 God's majestic position
v4-5 His spiritual heritage where God's power is displayed
v9 He was made by God and for Him
v10-11 From the very beginning of his life he relied on God and God never let him down
v19-21 He still believes that God is able to deliver him.

So here we have an expression of that profound experience of being entirely alone, knowing the truth but being unmoved by it; and that at the very time when God is needed most of all. That's what being forsaken means. That is common to many Christians, even those whom we admire most.

Maybe a pastoral reflection would help here. How do we deal with this when it comes along? Well, in my experience, Wesley's way is the best way. That is to say he was not at the mercy of his feelings. Feelings come and go. But our faith is not dependant on feelings. It depends on the finished work of Christ, not on how we feel about it. Evangelical Christians are very good at reminding us of the importance of feelings, but that is not the whole truth. Sometimes we just have to hold on in determined faith. It's the kind of thing that Charles Wesley meant when he wrote, 'I hold Thee with a trembling hand but will not let Thee go.' We need to trust Christ no matter what we feel and live a life of humble service believing that He will hold on to me when I cannot hold on to Him. Most of the time we may believe because of our feelings, but sometimes we need to believe in spite of them.

Here in Psalm 22 we have an account of the suffering of Christ. No one can fail to be impressed by the recurring references in the Psalm to His experience on Calvary. Verse 7 speaks of the insults thrown at Him. Verse 8 the mocking He endured, verse 15 His thirst, verse 16 the way His hands and feet were pierced and verse 18 the way others cast lots for His clothing. All summed up in the opening verse *'My God, my God, why have you forsaken me?'* Most significantly for our study – this is how those who first reflected on the death of Christ saw it. That is why they quoted this Psalm so often. Here, once again, they were looking at the cross through an Old Testament lens.

In recognising that Psalm 22 anticipates the sufferings of Christ we stumble across a most profound truth. It is that the experience of dereliction which we sometimes feel is not alien to God. In Christ He has borne that too. We are good at affirming that our sin was laid on Him. On the cross He took the dreadful consequence of human sin. Our iniquity was laid on Him. Yet that is not all He bore, for here we see Him identifying perfectly with the most profound experiences of the soul. He bears our pain, and confusion and all the tension which we feel when our theology does not match our experience. Our experiences fit Him perfectly. That is why He went through this. Here is vicarious suffering too. Christ voluntarily took it and offered it in humble sacrifice on the cross. The Father accepted it and transformed it from something terrible into a sign of hope for a lost world. How wonderfully the final paragraph of the Psalm speaks of the effect which this has had. **'The ends of the earth will remember and turn to the Lord'** (22:27). *'They will proclaim his righteousness to a people yet unborn – for he has done it'* (22:31).

I well remember David Watson and the impact which his ministry had on the church in Great Britain. I well remember too the devastating news that he had cancer. He spoke of the way people had written to him with an assurance that he would be healed. 'This sickness is not unto death' they quoted and they claimed that God had told them to tell him. Yet he died. That experience could be echoed a thousand times and more. This is not about a neat and tidy system of belief where everything works out just as it should. Quite the opposite. It is messy, and difficult and challenging. The cross is not about things turning out just as we think they ought. It is about Christ taking the heartbreak and confusion which we all know and crying out 'in a loud voice' to the God who is hidden when we need Him most.

David Watson recorded his own experiences in a lovely book called 'Fear no Evil'. As he recounts his struggle with terminal cancer he quotes Archbishop William Temple, and with this quote we conclude,

> 'There cannot be a God of love,' men say, 'because if there was, and he looked upon the world, his heart would break.' The Church points to the cross and says, 'It did break'. 'It is God who made the world', men say,' It is he who should bear the load.' The Church points to the cross and says, 'He did bear it.' Although Christ has suffered once for all on the cross for our sins, he still today weeps with those who weep, he feels our pain and enters into our sorrows with his compassionate love.'

AND FINALLY......

When the first followers of Jesus tried to make sense of the traumatic events surrounding His death and resurrection their understanding was shaped by their religious history. It was there that principles had been established which moulded their thinking and enabled them, not just to understand but also to interpret the events which they had witnessed. He was like a ram caught in a thicket, giving His life so that others may live. He was like a Passover lamb dying that others may escape judgement and go free. He was like a guilt offering, dying to remove the shadow which sin casts over our relationship with God. He was like a scapegoat, taking sin away so that it no longer had a claim on us. He was like a Suffering Servant, despised and rejected, who through His ignominious death bore the sins of many. He was like a confused believer crying out to the God in whom He believed but not getting an answer.

So when some of them came to record these momentous events they keep reminding us of the clues in their history which had shaped their understanding. It was as though, through long years God had been giving them hints which in the fullness of time bore fruit in their understanding of the cross. Their tools for making sense of the cross had been given over many generations and they used them to understand, interpret and proclaim the glorious truth of what God had done through the death of his Son.

But there is more….. When the New Testament writers quote the Old Testament in their passion narratives they do not speak of the events of the past as though they were clues which assisted their understanding; even though that may be a helpful way for us to think about them. Instead they use a very significant phrase. They say *'This was to fulfil scripture...'* or *'This happened that the scripture might be fulfilled....'* 'Fulfilled' is a very important word. It does not speak of a clue but a promise. Clues are discovered, but promises are fulfilled. So if they were right, and I'm sure they were, God had not been dropping clues for them to discover, but making promises which He would later fulfil. This shifts our thinking, because instead of placing the emphasis on the writer's perception it places it on God's provision. If God had been making promises then it places Him in control of the whole thing. It means that unfolding history had been working towards this momentous event. It had been in God's mind and heart from the very beginning. This was the way, the only way, to win back a lost world for Himself, to restore a broken relationship, to bring wayward sinners home. The cross is the fulcrum of history. Everything turns on this. It did not happen because the religious leaders were against Him, or because the disciples left Him, or because Pilate acquiesced in administering justice, or because soldiers drove nails through His hands and feet. It happened because this was God's way of redeeming a lost world and changing your life for ever. On a lonely hillside outside the city wall Jesus died on a cross and it was done! The promise of history had been fulfilled. God had done the most costly thing imaginable. The offer was made. Now it's up to you!